Animal Rights

Distinguishing Between Fact and Opinion

Curriculum Consultant: JoAnne Buggey, Ph.D.
College of Education, University of Minnesota

By Bradley Steffens

Greenhaven Press, Inc.
Post Office Box 289009
San Diego, CA 92128-9009

Titles in the opposing viewpoints juniors series:

Smoking	Death Penalty
Gun Control	Drugs and Sports
Animal Rights	Toxic Wastes
AIDS	Patriotism
Alcohol	Working Mothers
Immigration	Terrorism

Cover photo: © J. Barry O'Rourke

Library of Congress Cataloging-in-Publication Data

Animal rights : distinguishing between fact and opinion / [edited] by
  Brad Steffens ; curriculum consultant, JoAnne Buggey.
    p. cm. — (Opposing viewpoints juniors)
    Summary: Presents opposing viewpoints on the treatment of
animals. Includes critical thinking skill activities.
    ISBN 0-89908-471-0
    1. Animals, Treatment of—Juvenile literature. [1. Animals—
Treatment.   2. Critical thinking.]   1. Steffens, Brad, 1956–
II. Series.
HV4711.A57 1990
179'.3—dc20   89-2200
                                                                                CIP
                                                                                 AC

CONTENTS

An Introduction to
Opposing Viewpoints

When people disagree, it is hard to figure out who is right. You may decide one person is right just because the person is your friend or relative. But this is not a very good reason to agree or disagree with someone. It is better if you try to understand why these people disagree. On what main points do the two people disagree? Read or listen to each person's argument carefully. Separate the facts and opinions that each person presents. Finally, decide which argument best matches what you think. This process, examining an argument without emotion, is part of what critical thinking is all about.

This is not easy. Many things make it hard to understand and form opinions. People's values, age, and experience all influence the way they think. This is why learning to read and think critically is an invaluable skill. Opposing Viewpoints Juniors books will help

you learn and practice skills to improve your ability to read critically. By reading opposing views on an issue, you will become familiar with methods people use to attempt to convince you that their point of view is right. And you will learn to separate the authors' opinions from the facts they present.

Each Opposing Viewpoints Juniors book focuses on one critical thinking skill that will help you judge the views presented. Some of these skills are telling fact from opinion, recognizing propaganda techniques, and locating and analyzing the main idea. These skills will allow you to examine opposing viewpoints more easily. Each viewpoint is paraphrased from the original to make it easier to read. The viewpoints are placed in a running debate and are always placed with the pro view first.

What Is the Difference Between Fact and Opinion?

In this Opposing Viewpoints Juniors book you will be asked to identify and study statements of fact and statements of opinion. A fact is a statement that can be proved true. Here are some examples of factual statements: "The Statue of Liberty was dedicated in 1886 in New York," "Dinosaurs are extinct," and "George Washington was the first U.S. president." It is a fairly easy thing to prove these facts true. For instance, a historian in the year 3000 might need to prove when the Statue of Liberty was dedicated. One way she might do this is to check in the Hall of Records in New York. She would try to find a source to verify the date. Sometimes it is harder to prove facts true. And some ideas that are stated as facts may not be. In this book you will be asked to question facts presented in the viewpoints and be given some ways in which you might go about proving them.

Statements of opinion cannot be proved. An opinion is a statement that expresses how a person feels about something or what a person thinks is true. Remember the facts we mentioned? They can easily be changed into statements of opinion. For example, "Dinosaurs became extinct because a huge meteor hit the Earth," "George Washington was the best president the United States ever had," and "Rebuilding the Statue of Liberty was a waste of money," are all statements of opinion. They express what one person believes to be true. Opinions are not better than facts. They are different. Opinions are based on many things, including religious,

social, moral, and family values. Opinions can also be based on medical and scientific facts. For instance, many scientists have made intelligent guesses about other planets based on what they know is true about Earth. The only way these scientists would know their opinions were right is if they were able to visit other planets and test their guesses. Until their guesses are proved, then, they remain opinions. Some people have opinions that we do not like, or with which we disagree. That does not always make their opinions wrong—or right. There is room in our world for many different opinions.

When you read differing views on any issue, it is very important to know when people are using facts and when they are using opinions in an argument. When writers use facts, it makes their argument more believable and easier to prove. The more facts the author has, the more the reader can tell that the writer's opinion is based on something other than personal feelings.

Authors that base their arguments mostly on their own opinions, then, are impossible to prove factually true.

This does not mean that these types of argument are not as meaningful. It means that you, as the reader, must decide whether or not you agree or disagree based on personal reasons, not factual ones.

We asked two students to give their opinions on the animal rights issue. Examine the following viewpoints. Look for facts and opinions in their arguments.

I think animals should have rights.

They are like us in many ways. Many animals take care of their babies. Some animals mate for life. Dolphins can talk to each other. And whales have bigger brains than we do.

Instead of treating animals like us, we do terrible things to them. We put them in zoos. We experiment on them in laboratories. We kill them and eat them. What gives us the right to treat animals like slaves?

I think that my dog Emer deserves more rights than some people do. She has never hurt anyone or stolen anything. But if she ever got lost, she would be taken to a dog pound. If no one came to get her, she would be killed. Even our worst criminals have more rights than that.

We treat bad people better than we treat good animals. That isn't fair. It isn't right.

I don't think animals should have rights.

Treating animals like people is stupid. I love my cat Chaos but if I had to choose between saving her life or saving my brother's life, I would save my brother. A kid's life is worth more than an animal's.

People use animals to help other people. By using animals in research, scientists can cure diseases that kill people. We also need to use animals for food. If we didn't eat animals and fish, more people would starve.

Some animals must also kill to survive. Lions eat zebras. Whales eat plankton. Mosquitoes eat our blood! Animals don't care about our rights. They just survive. We should do the same.

I like animals. I think they should be treated well. Endangered animals should be protected so they don't become extinct. But animals should not be treated as our equals. Human beings are more important.

Zeke and Tessa have very different opinions about animal rights. Both use facts and opinions in their arguments:

Zeke:

FACTS

Many animals take care of their babies.

Whales have bigger brains than humans.

OPINIONS

Animals should have rights.

We treat bad people better than we treat good animals.

Tessa:

FACTS

By using animals in research, scientists can cure diseases.

Lions eat zebras.

OPINIONS

A kid's life is worth more than an animal's.

We should do the same.

In this sample, Zeke and Tessa have an equal number of facts and opinions. Zeke's facts are based on things he has read or heard about animals. Tessa's facts are based on things she has read or heard about people. What conclusions would you come to from this sample? Why?

Think of two facts and two opinions you have about animal rights. As you read the viewpoints in this book, keep a tally like the one above to compare the authors' arguments.

CHAPTER 1

PREFACE: How Important Are Animal Rights?

Almost everyone agrees that animals should be treated kindly, but some people, called animal rights activists, believe that animals deserve more than kind treatment. These people believe that animals should have the same rights as human beings.

The first two viewpoints in this book debate the question of whether animals should have rights. The first author reasons that the rights of all creatures, including animals, should be protected at any cost. The second author states that humans should put their needs above animals' rights, without feeling shame or guilt.

As you read these viewpoints, look for the facts and opinions each author presents. Which case is more strongly based on fact?

Animal rights are more important than human needs

Editor's Note: This viewpoint is paraphrased from an article by Lawrence Finsen, a professor of philosophy at the University of Redlands in California. Mr. Finsen reasons that if animals are similar enough to humans to be useful in experiments, they are also similar enough to humans to deserve equal rights.

What fact does the author state to make his point that many animal tests are useless?

Many people believe that animals should not be used in research experiments. Other people disagree. They argue that human health needs are more important than animal rights. But this argument does not tell the whole truth. Sixty million animals die in U.S. labs each year. But only a few are used for research into diseases such as cancer. Millions of animals die for such useless reasons as the testing of products like cosmetics and shampoo. These tests are done even though safe products already are in use.

Other research *is* aimed at improving human health, but it is not necessary. For example, we know that cigarette smoking is a health hazard. But laboratory animals are still forced to inhale cigarette smoke.

Is this a fact or an opinion? Why?

This kind of testing continues because most people believe humans are more important than animals. This has been a common belief for a long time, but in the last 150 years this view has begun to change. Scientists like Charles Darwin have shown that human beings are like animals in many ways. In fact, a great deal of animal research (such as pain studies) is valuable *because* humans and animals are so alike. Both animals and people are able to feel pain and suffering. We are the same in this way. The idea the humans are superior to animals is based on prejudice, not scientific fact.

THE WIZARD OF ID By Brant Parker and Johnny Hart

By permission of Johnny Hart and NAS, Inc.

Since we know that animals can feel pain, many people are asking if humans have the right to make animals suffer. This is not to say that humans should never hurt or kill an animal. It simply means that we must have good reasons for doing it. It is not enough to say that we will benefit in some way from animal research. Once we agree that we need good reasons to hurt animals, we see that much of what we do to animals is wrong.

We live in a world that takes advantage of animals on a mass scale. We use animals not only for research, but also for food (meat), clothing (leather shoes), sports (rodeos), and entertainment (zoos and circuses). The law is on the side of human beings. Animals enjoy almost no protection and certainly no legal rights. This is why some animal rights activists break the law to make their point, raiding laboratories and destroying property. Those who condemn such actions should help improve the lot of animals in laboratories.

Why does the author say people need to have good reasons to hurt animals? Is this a fact or an opinion?

Is this a fact or an opinion?

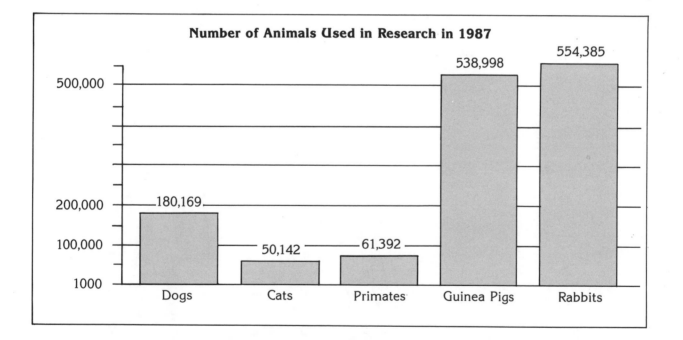

Number of Animals Used in Research in 1987

Dogs	180,169
Cats	50,142
Primates	61,392
Guinea Pigs	538,998
Rabbits	554,385

Are animals equal to humans?

Mr. Finsen says that science has shown animals to be like humans. What two examples does he give to prove his point? Are these examples facts or opinions?

ANIMAL RIGHTS   **11**

2 Animal rights are not more important than human needs

Editor's Note: This viewpoint is paraphrased from an article by Tibor R. Machan, a professor of philosophy at Auburn University in Alabama. He argues that animals are not equal to humans. He also suggests that giving rights to animals could harm humans.

Do animals deserve the same rights as human beings? If so, then the government should protect animals from being killed or used against their will. If we believe that animals have rights, we should stop eating animals and experimenting on them. But is this wise?

The animals liberation movement argues that animals are no different from humans, except that they cannot speak out for themselves. But this is an important difference. It shows that animals do not have free will. They do not choose how to behave. If animals received rights like ours, they would not know what to do with them.

Giving animals rights like ours would create new problems. For example, animals kill each other; would the law require that animals be tried for murder in a court of law? If so, who would serve as judge and jury?

Is this a fact or an opinion? Why?

"Sure it looks easy! But if you get to the cheese, they try to give you cancer!"

Reprinted by permission, The American Legion Magazine, copyright 1986.

It is not silly to ask such questions because animals rights activists are not talking simply about kindness to animals. They are talking about full rights and freedoms.

I agree that human beings should be kind to animals and take care of them. But caring is one thing and rights are another. Human beings are part of nature, and we must make use of nature for our own benefit, even pleasure. It would be a mistake to feel guilty about our use of animals. This guilt might lead some of us to support movements, like animal liberation, that would end our happiness on earth. We should admit proudly that we value ourselves more than animals, then treat animals with care and concern. This would be best not only for us but also for the animals.

The author says humans should not feel guilty about using animals. Why not? Are his reasons based on fact or opinion?

"We're putting miners down the mine shaft to make sure it's safe for canaries..."

Reprinted with permission.

Are humans superior to animals?

Mr. Machan names one way in which animals are different from humans. What is it? Do you agree with the author that humans are superior to animals? Why or why not?

Tallying the Facts and Opinions

After reading the two viewpoints on animal rights, make a chart similar to the one made for Zeke and Tessa on page 8. List the facts and opinions each author gives to make his case. A chart is started for you below:

Finsen:

FACTS

Sixty million animals die in research laboratories.

OPINIONS

Some research is not needed.

Machan:

FACTS

Animals cannot speak for themselves.

OPINIONS

Animals do not choose how to behave.

Which article used more factual statements? Which was more convincing? Which did you personally agree with? Why? List some facts and opinions that had influenced your opinion before you read the articles.

2

PREFACE: Should Animals Be Used in Research Experiments?

Every year, millions of animals are used in laboratories for tests that are supposed to benefit people. The purpose of some of this research is to discover new drugs and learn about diseases. Other tests are performed to find if products are safe to use. Almost every test takes away the animals' freedom to move about or eat as they wish. Often, the tests cause pain, sometimes even death.

The following authors debate whether using animals in experiments is right. Both use facts and opinions to support their arguments. The questions in the margins will help you decide if some statements are facts or opinions.

Editor's Note: This viewpoint is paraphrased from an article by Michael Allen Fox, a professor of philosophy at Queen's University in Ontario, Canada. Mr. Fox argues that animal rights activists overlook a simple truth: human beings are more important than animals.

The author argues that people are aware of only one side of animal research. Is this a fact or an opinion?

Is this a fact or an opinion?

People like you and I must decide the future of animal research. Unfortunately, most people hear only the side of the argument that says all animals—including humans—are equal. People who oppose animal research describe animal suffering, but they do not discuss the benefits gained from animal research. Meanwhile, TV and newspapers report only the emotional appeals made on behalf of animals and show pictures of animals saved in raids on laboratories. These acts are meant to shock people and make them feel there is something "wrong" with animal research. That is why it is important to give reasons for something most people have believed for thousands of years—that animals are not our equals, and there is no reason to treat them as such.

Most of us can see that animals are capable of suffering. Some animals are very much like us in important ways. Every day, cruel things are done to animals around the world. These acts are wrong. The fact that they take place must to be taken into account as we think about the use and treatment of animals. But that does not mean that we have to change our belief that animals are not our equals.

Perhaps we should ask what counts as an "animal." Lions, whales, zebras, and mice surely are. So are oysters, ants, butterflies, and mosquitoes, if we stretch our concept a bit. But what about viruses, bacteria, and other single-cell creatures? Where do we draw the line? The animal kingdom includes species that do not have a nervous system (amoebas, sea cucumbers, certain mollusks). It includes those that are conscious of some things (fish, insects, reptiles, birds). And it includes those with large brains and a wide range of social and problem-solving abilities (chimpanzees, dolphins, humans). How much concern we have for each species surely depends on how smart we think it is.

Is this a fact or an opinion?

Those who support animal rights often ask, "What *right* do we have to experiment on animals?" This is a question we should not even have to answer. We do not need a special right to experiment on animals. Since animals are not our equals, there is no moral reason to keep us from using them as we wish. In fact, I believe it would be wrong *not* to use animals if using them is the only way to end some kinds of human and animal suffering.

Is this a fact or an opinion? Do you agree?

I believe that the energy used for animal rights would be better spent trying to make things better for people. In fact, focusing on animals takes attention away from human problems. My point is not that people should work twenty-four hours a day to improve human welfare. That is impossible. My point is that human welfare is more important than animal welfare. Relieving human need and suffering is vital to the survival of our species; the welfare of animals is not.

Animals used for research in 1986 and some of the benefits—	
Primates 49,000	AIDS research, vaccine development, studies of Alzheimer's and Parkinson's diseases
Cats 54,000	Vision research
Dogs 180,000	Heart-surgery research
Rats, mice 12-15,000,000	Cancer research, safety testing of new drugs

SOURCE: U.S. Dept. of Agriculture

Are humans more important than animals?

The author believes humans are more important than animals. He believes this is why experimenting on animals is alright. Do you agree with him? Why or why not?

Editor's Note: This viewpoint is paraphrased from the book *The Case for Animal Rights* by Tom Regan. Mr. Regan is a professor of philosophy at North Carolina State University. He calls his philosophy of animal rights "the rights view," which states that animals have the same basic rights as humans.

Is this a fact or an opinion? Why?

What fact does the author use to show that testing beauty products on animals is unnecessary?

Is this a fact or an opinion? Why?

I believe all forms of life have the right to live freely. This belief is called "the rights view." Tests on animals take these rights away. Such tests should be stopped.

Some people say that products can only be tested by using animals. This is false. Beauty Without Cruelty is a product testing group that does not use animals. Its work proves it is possible to make safe cosmetics without testing them on animals.

Some people agree that animals should not be used to test beauty products, but they claim that testing new drugs is different. They argue that human lives may be lost if we fail to search for causes and cures for diseases. They claim that if we do not test new drugs on animals first, we will not know if these products are safe for humans.

Anyone who takes a new drug runs the risk that the drug may not be safe. That is the person's choice. To force animals to take the drug to see if it is safe violates their rights. The question is not how much test animals are harmed, or even if they are harmed at all. What matters is that they are not allowed to choose for themselves. It is true that people would run greater risks if drugs were not tested. But people can choose to avoid taking a drug if they feel it is unsafe.

BLOOM COUNTY by Berke Breathed. © 1988, Washington Post Writers Group. Reprinted with permission.

Some people call the rights view "antihuman." This is false. The rights view does not say that the rights of humans should be taken away for the good of animals. But the rights of animals should not be taken away for the good of humans, either.

People also say the right view is antiscientific. This is also false. The rights view challenges scientists to find new ways to answer medical and scientific questions. For example, whatever we can learn from treating sick animals or humans should be used. But animals should not be burned, shocked, poisoned, or starved just to see what we might learn.

The rights view is not against research on animals if it does not harm them. This does not mean merely making sure test animals receive drugs to ease their suffering or are kept in clean cages with enough food and water. It is not only pain that matters. It is the harm done to animals. This includes limiting their freedom.

It is not clear if harmless research is possible. That being so, any research that uses animals should be stopped. Tests that do not use animals should be used. If they are not available, they should be found. Scientists who say this cannot be done show a lack of belief in science. They are stating something as a fact before testing to see if it is true.

The rights view is not antiscientific. It is only opposed to those scientific practices that take away animal rights. If that means there are some things we cannot learn, so be it. There are also things we cannot learn because we refuse to experiment on humans. The rights view only asks that humans and animals be treated with equal respect.

Is this a fact or an opinion?

Name two opinions the author offers to support his view that animal testing should be stopped.

Humans and risk

Mr. Regan gives one reason why humans should take the risk of trying new medicines. What is it? Is this reason fact or opinion? Why? Do you agree with Mr. Regan that humans, not animals, should take this risk? Why or why not?

2

Understanding Editorial Cartoons

Throughout this book, cartoons illustrate the ideas in the viewpoints. Editorial cartoons are an effective way to give an opinion because they are fun to read and easy to remember. While many cartoons are easy to understand, some, like the one pictured below, require more thought.

The cartoon below deals with the use of animals in laboratory tests. It is similar to the cartoons that appear in your daily newspaper. According to the cartoon, what do scientists care more about, animals or product testing? What opinion does the cartoon present about animal experimentation? How can you tell?

For further practice, look at the editorial cartoons in your daily newspaper. Identify the cartoons' opinions. See if you can find a cartoon that uses a fact to back up its opinion.

"I'm sorry they're dead, but at least it proves that one powder washes whiter than the other."

© Punch/Rothco

CHAPTER

3

PREFACE: Should Animals Be Used for Food?

In the U.S., most people eat meat. We have a large meat producing industry that raises millions of chickens, cattle, and other animals to be consumed by humans. Although meat eating is widely accepted, some people refuse to eat meat. They believe that killing animals for human food is morally wrong. They also argue that it is unnecessary.

Both of the following writers use numbers, called statistics, to support their views. Pay close attention to these statistics. You will be asked about them in the Critical Thinking Skill that follows the viewpoints.

VIEWPOINT 5 Animals should be used for food

Editor's Note: This viewpoint is paraphrased from the book *The Meat We Eat* by John Romans. Mr. Romans is an associate professor of animal science at the University of Illinois. He argues that eating meat is a healthy practice that makes wise use of the world's resources.

The author uses two statistics to prove his point. Do you think they support his opinion? Why or why not?

Is this a fact or an opinion?

Eating animals is a good way to use the world's food resources. Nearly one third of the world's agricultural land cannot produce crops people can eat. In the United States, 44 percent of the total land area produces grass and vegetation that cattle, sheep, goats, and deer can digest, but humans cannot. The only way for people to obtain food from this land is to eat the animals that feed on it.

The ability to convert grass and grain into food for humans has made flocks and herds important in the development of civilization. Meat is always the main food for settlers of new lands. A large supply of meat is associated with a happy, active people.

Americans spend more than $50 billion dollars on meat each year. How much meat people eat depends on their income and meat prices. The old expression "no money, no meat" still holds true. Those in the middle income range eat the most meat, especially if their jobs require a lot of physical work. Youths eat most of the hamburgers and hot dogs.

We are able to digest the nutrients in meat because meat is very much like human body tissue. Other foods contain important food elements, but our bodies cannot digest them easily. The ability of a food to be used by the human body is known as its *biological value.* Meat has a high biological value.

People understood the merits of meat long before scientists described biological value. This was expressed in the saying "meat sticks to the ribs."

Is this saying a fact or an opinion?

Meat contains all ten amino acids needed for human life, and its proteins are complete. It contains all the minerals the human body needs (except calcium). It also is rich in vitamins. The fat in meat offers more than twice as much energy as carbohydrates.

The completeness of meat as a food is apparent in the health of Eskimos. They survive almost solely on meat. It provides the strength and energy they need to live in a very hostile climate.

Are these statements facts or opinions? Are they good reasons to eat meat?

Brushing aside all that has been said, let us look at plain, hungry people seated around a table. By instinct, we look for the platter of meat. To most of us, it is not only the king, but the whole royal family of appetite appeal. It has more aroma than any other foods, causing our mouths to water. As we bite into it, we receive a pleasant feeling. As we swallow, satisfaction shows in our eyes, our speech, our actions. We become friendlier and more clear-minded—high tribute to a food product.

Are these statements facts or opinions? Do they prove that eating meat is right?

Meat as food

The author bases his case for eating meat on its importance and goodness as a food for people. Name two reasons the author gives that prove meat is nutritious. Do you believe they are good reasons to eat meat? Why or why not?

Editor's Note: This viewpoint is paraphrased from the book *In Defense of Animals.* The author is Harriet Schleifer, an editor for the animal rights magazine called *Animals' Agenda.* She believes that all people should become vegetarians—people who do not eat meat. She maintains that eating meat takes away animals' rights and wastes the world's resources.

What statistics does the author use to prove that people eat a lot of meat?

Is this a fact or an opinion? Why?

What is the author's point about advertising? Is her point a fact or an opinion?

Are these statements facts or opinions?

Every society on earth raises animals for food. Billions of animals are slaughtered each year. In the U.S., the meat industry is second in size only to the automobile industry. Americans spend $50 billion a year on meat, poultry, and fish.

Even though the meat industry is large, it fears the public's concern for animals. As a result, meat producers do many things to hide the true nature of their work. Factory farms are located away from cities. Most do not allow visitors. Meat is sold in neat, bloodless packets. Body parts—feet, tails, fur, eyes—are carefully removed.

Slick advertising supports the illusion. Living, suffering animals are not shown. Instead, dancing pigs, smiling cows, and laughing chickens appear on meat, dairy, and egg packaging.

Special advertising is aimed at children. The McDonald's hamburger chain is a major producer of children's TV commercials. In one of these, Ronald McDonald explains that hamburgers "grow in little hamburger patches." In Star-Kist ads, Charlie the Tuna tries to be caught so he can be processed by the company.

BLOOM COUNTY by Berke Breathed. © 1988 Washington Post Writers Group. Reprinted with permission.

Animal rights demands a change in our thinking about meat. We cannot think about meat without thinking of the animals used to produce it. We do not believe humans are superior to animals. We respect all living beings. The vegetarian lifestyle is a way of showing this respect.

The case for vegetarianism becomes even stronger for reasons that do not relate to farm animals. Many people care about protecting wildlife, but few realize that farm animals compete with wild animals for space and resources. Ninety percent of farm land is used for meat, dairy, and egg operations. This land is unavailable to wild animals. Those in the meat industry also harm wildlife that threatens their animals. American ranchers kill wolves, coyotes, antelope, and prairie dogs. Australian sheep farmers kill kangaroos. Japanese fishermen destroy dolphins.

Raising animals for food is wasteful and inefficient. Animals require ten to one thousand times more water and energy than plants to produce the same amount of food. If all meat eaters became vegetarians, it would be possible for every starving person in the world to receive four tons of grain.

Some animal rights activists call for kinder slaughter. This suggests that the killing is not a problem, only the way it is done. This is wrong. Meat is murder. If an animal loses the right to exist, other rights are meaningless.

Raising farm animals is an unnatural process. It enslaves animals and subjects them to our will. Animal liberation would return domestic animals to their wild origins, free to live without human interference.

What fact does the author use to prove that meat production hurts wildlife?

What fact does the author use to prove that raising animals is wasteful?

Is this a fact or an opinion? Why?

Is this a fact or an opinion? Why?

Name two reasons the author gives to support her view that raising animals for food is wrong. Are they facts or opinions? Why?

Is eating meat wrong?

Ms. Schleifer says that eating meat is wrong. Do you agree or disagree? Why? What shaped your opinion: your family, your religion, meat advertising, or something you have read?

3 Distinguishing Between Fact and Opinion

This activity will allow you to practice distinguishing between fact and opinion. The statements below focus on the subject matter of this chapter, whether or not animals should be used for food. Read each statement and consider it carefully. *Mark O for any statement you believe is an opinion, or what one person believes to be true. Mark F for any statement you believe is a fact, or something that can be proven to be true. Mark U for any statement for which you cannot decide.*

If you are doing this activity as a member of a class or group, compare your answers with other class or group members. You will find that others may have different answers than you do. Listening to the reasons others give for their answers can help you in distinguishing fact from opinion.

EXAMPLE: Most people in the U.S. eat meat.

ANSWER: Fact: This statement could be proven by looking at statistics that show how much meat is sold in the U.S.

answer

1. Eating animals is the only way to keep healthy. _____

2. A vegetarian is a person who does not eat meat. _____

3. In stores, meat is sold in clean, bloodless packages. _____

4. People who eat meat are unhealthy. _____

5. Meat is murder. _____

6. Americans spend 50 billion dollars a year on meat. _____

7. If everyone stopped eating meat, everyone in the world would have enough food. _____

8. Cattle and sheep use land that wild animals need. _____

4

PREFACE: Does Hunting Harm Wildlife?

Humans have always hunted animals. Since the invention of the gun, however, hunters have been able to kill many more animals than ever before. Whole herds of buffalo, deer, and antelope have been wiped out. Since then, laws have been passed to limit hunting and preserve wildlife.

The following authors debate whether hunting as it is practiced today endangers wildlife or helps to protect it.

Again the authors use statistics to support their arguments. Watch to see if the statistics support the opinions.

Editor's Note: This viewpoint is paraphrased from a pamphlet published by the National Shooting Sports Foundation Inc., an association of gun owners. The Foundation argues that hunters help wildlife survive.

Is this conclusion based on fact or opinion? How can you tell?

The author uses the term "harvesting" for hunting. Why?

Is this a fact of an opinion?

Many people believe that hunting should not be allowed. These people think that if there were no hunters, animals could live in peace, and the forests would be filled with wildlife. This would not happen. If hunters are not allowed to kill some animals, then nature kills them in a cruel, harsh way.

After a deer herd eats all available food in winter, some deer in the herd slowly starve to death. Predators kill young and weak animals. Disease and parasites take the lives of even more. The herd becomes weak and unhealthy. This herd would have more deer if hunters were allowed to kill some of them.

Research shows that a healthy herd can lose 40 percent of its members with no ill effect on its future population. Yet in most states, hunters rarely harvest more than 15 percent of the deer.

The benefit of harvesting wild animals is even more evident with game birds. Each year, 75 to 80 percent of quail die whether they are hunted or not. The number of doves and pheasants is also limited by natural factors. The availability of food and shelter and the severity of the weather affect them more than hunting does.

Hunters play a useful role in taking care of wildlife. They help improve animal environments. And they hunt only during certain seasons. That way, they harvest only extra animals.

Each state has a fish and game department. These departments have thousands of people working for them. These people work for the well-being of birds, animals, and fish. Their work affects millions of acres of land and costs hundreds of millions of dollars every year.

Almost all of the money for fish and game departments comes from selling licenses and stamps to hunters. Since 1920, hunters have paid $5 billion into wildlife programs. Currently, hunters pay $400 million a year. This money is spent on projects that increase wildlife. These projects benefit not just hunters but all Americans who enjoy seeing wild animals.

By funding preservation programs with their money, hunters have helped increase the numbers of many kinds of wild animals. For example, only forty-five years ago, the total number of pronghorn antelope in the United States was about twelve thousand. Today, there are more than one million. The money for the antelope conservation program came mainly from hunters.

The same is true for other animals. In 1920, there were only 500,000 white-tailed deer in the entire country. Now there are sixteen million. The national population of wild turkeys has increased from 97,000 in 1952 to over two million today.

The fact is that no game bird or animal is endangered by hunters. Rather, it is the helping hand of the sportsman that will protect and preserve wildlife so it can be enjoyed by future generations.

Is this a fact or an opinion?

Is this a fact or an opinion?

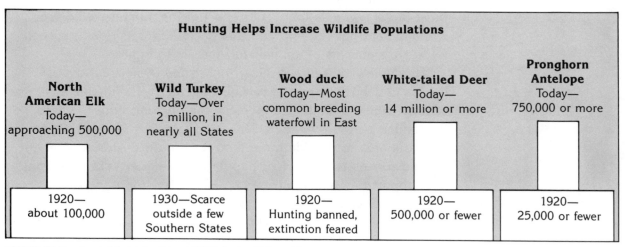

Hunting Helps Increase Wildlife Populations

North American Elk
Today—approaching 500,000
1920—about 100,000

Wild Turkey
Today—Over 2 million, in nearly all States
1930—Scarce outside a few Southern States

Wood duck
Today—Most common breeding waterfowl in East
1920—Hunting banned, extinction feared

White-tailed Deer
Today—14 million or more
1920—500,000 or fewer

Pronghorn Antelope
Today—750,000 or more
1920—25,000 or fewer

SOURCE: U.S. Department of the Interior, Fish and Wildlife Service, *50 Years of Restoring America's Wildlife, 1937–1982.*

Do hunters help wildlife?

The author states that if hunters do not kill animals, then nature will. Is this a fact or an opinion? Do you believe it is a good reason to allow hunting? Why or why not?

Editor's Note: This viewpoint is paraphrased from an article by Luke A. Dommer, head of the Committee to Abolish Sports Hunting. Mr. Dommer argues that hunting destroys not only animals but also the land on which they live.

Is this a fact or an opinion? Why?

Hunters argue that animals die from starvation, disease, and predators when hunting is not used to manage wildlife. They say that hunting helps to keep wildlife in balance with available food and shelter. This is the basic reason given in support of hunting, but it ignores the facts.

The animal population is controlled by natural factors. These factors include food, space, predators, parasites, and disease. If one factor changes, other factors keep the population within certain limits. According to Wayne Evans, Ph.D., assistant director of the New Mexico Fish and Game Commission, "Hunting has never been necessary for population control."

In 1842, the United States Supreme Court declared: "Wildlife is held in trust for all citizens." This means that the government must protect wildlife for all citizens, not just hunters. Wildlife management has not followed this declaration. Its goal has been to create a surplus of animals for hunters to hunt.

This policy caused a disaster in Arizona. A herd of four thousand deer lived on the Kaibab Plateau in the nineteenth century. Hunters wanted to increase the population of the herd, so they killed all the predators. They also removed 195,000 sheep from the area to provide more food for the deer. This experiment worked so well that the deer population exploded. The land could not support this many deer. As a result, sixty thousand deer starved to death.

"Why don't they thin their own damned herd?"

State agencies have created a population of sixteen million deer. This is a disaster. To create such a surplus of deer, state agencies practice a method called controlled burning. Burning grass and forest creates more grass for the deer, and more deer for the hunter. However, it also roasts alive countless non-game animals that non-hunters would enjoy seeing. It also leads to over-grazing. Controlled burning and over-grazing have made eight million acres of forests barren. Rabbits, song birds, and other species are vanishing because the land cannot support them.

I have not gone into the issue of who is paying for wildlife conservation. But rest assured, the hunters are only paying a small part of the bill. Most of the money comes from taxes paid by everyone.

If hunting were ended, animals would adapt to the end of hunting by changing diet or having fewer young. For deer, the immediate effect would be over-grazing, damage to crops, starvation, and worse health for the population. But within several years, the population would reach a level in balance with the supply of food. The new population would be healthier than the old one. This is because natural thinning would kill more of the old and sick animals than would the hunter.

Hunters want non-hunters to believe that they take the place of natural predators. We all know that natural predators remove the unfit animals from the herd. This helps the herd survive. Now who could believe that the modern day hunter would hunt down a sick and diseased animal to take home for dinner? In fact, hunting hurts the herd because it kills its healthiest members.

Human beings should not support the crippling and killing of millions of innocent and defenseless animals in the name of recreation. If we do, we cannot claim to be more noble than animals. At least they do not kill for fun.

More harm than good?

The author describes several ways hunters hurt wildlife. Give two facts and two opinions from the viewpoint that show how. After reading this viewpoint and the previous one, what do you conclude about hunting? Give one fact and one opinion in support of your own view.

CRITICAL THINKING SKILL 4

Analyzing Hunting Advertising

This activity will help you analyze the different messages portrayed in two ads about hunting.

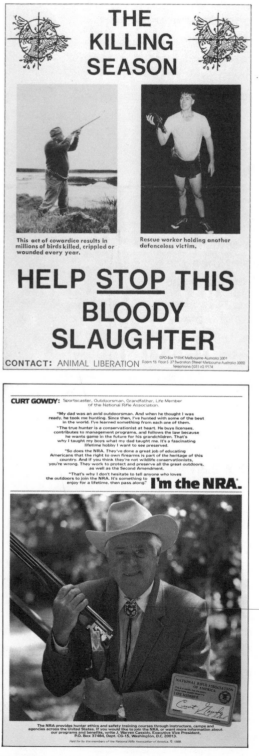

PART I

Examine ad number one. What message do you think the Animal Liberation group is giving in its poster? Examine the two photos. What is the group's opinion of the hunter? What kind of words in the headline pop out to tell you that this group is against hunting? Do you think this poster is effective? Would your attitude about hunting be changed by this ad? Why or why not?

Now look at ad number two. It is an advertisement for the National Rifle Association, an organization that supports hunting. What is its message? How does it contrast with the message in ad number one? Why is the picture of the man used? Read the text. What impression does it give you of hunters? Do you think the ad is effective? Would this ad change your mind if you were a non-hunter? Why or why not? After looking at both ads, decide which message you would pay more attention to. Why?

PART II

Write some factual statements expressed by the messages in the ads.

EXAMPLE: Millions of birds are killed each year by hunters.

Write some opinionated statements the ads convey.

EXAMPLE: Ad number two suggests hunters are cowards.